A Family Life Nature Series

The Gospel According to a THORNLESS BLACKBERRY

By Terry & Jean McComb

Illustrations by Vera McMurdo

TEACH Services, Inc.
PUBLISHING
www.TEACHServices.com • (800) 367-1844

World rights reserved. Portions of this book may be photocopied for evangelistic purposes.

The author assumes full responsibility for the accuracy of all facts and quotations as cited in this book. The opinions expressed in this book are the author's personal views and interpretations, and do not necessarily reflect those of the publisher.

This book is provided with the understanding that the publisher is not engaged in giving spiritual, legal, medical, or other professional advice. If authoritative advice is needed, the reader should seek the counsel of a competent professional.

All rights reserved. No part of this publication may be reproduced, stored in a retrieval system, or transmitted in any form or by any means, except for brief quotations in printed reviews, without the prior permission of the publisher. Portions of this book may be photocopied for evangelistic purposes.

Copyright© 2023 Terry & Jean McComb
Copyright© 2023 TEACH Services, Inc.
ISBN-13: 978-1-4796-1242-0 (Paperback)
ISBN-13: 978-1-4796-1243-7 (ePub)
Library of Congress Control Number: 2022949418

Any personal website addresses that the author included are managed by the author. TEACH Services is not responsible for the accuracy or permanency of any links.

Scripture taken from the New King James Version®. Copyright © 1982 by Thomas Nelson. Used by permission. All rights reserved. Italics omitted.

Illustrations by Vera McMurdo

Published by

www.TEACHServices.com • (800) 367-1844

Table of Contents

Page	Nature Object	Text	Character Lesson
v	Preface		
6	Briars and Thorns	Genesis 3:17–18; Matthew 13:28	Why Suffering
8	Law of Genetics	Galatians 6:7–9; Romans 12:21	Reap and Sow
10	Cultivation	Ephesians 4:22-24	Choose Good
12	Culling Out	Romans 6:11, 13	Power of Choice
14	Thornless Bushes…But Yucky Fruit	Matthew 7:16	Bad Goodness
16	Patient Cross-Breeding	Romans 5:19; Romans 8:24–25	Hope
18	Spiritual Law of Genetics	Exodus 20:12	Obey Parents
20	Stubborn Thorns	Romans 7; Deuteronomy 6:2	Patience
22	Seeds	Mark 4:26–27	Multiplication
24	Clean Garden	Matthew 13:40-42	Clear Conscience
26	Slow Growth, Needs TIME	Romans 5:2-5	Endurance Hope
28	Slow Growth Wait	Romans 8:24, 25	Perseverance
30	Full Fruit on Thornless Bushes	Galatians 6:14; Revelation 14:4	Assurance
32	Plant Timing	Ecclesiastes 3:1	Stages of Growth
34	Delicious Fruit on Thornless Bushes	Ephesians 3:16-21; 2 Corinthians 4:7, 11, 16	Glorification, 2nd Coming
36	First Fruit Love	1 John 4:19	Receive Love
38	Love and Joy	Galatians 5:22	Family Love; Delight
40	Peace and Patience	Galatians 5:22	Peace, Patience
42	Gentle Kindness and Goodness	Galatians 5:22	Sibling Rivalry; Helpers
44	Faith and Gentle Meekness	Galatians 5:22	Parenting
46	Self-Control	Galatians 5:22	Good for Evil
48	Pruning	James 4:10; 2 Timothy 3:16–17	Reproof
50	Where Blackberries Grow Best	Matthew 10:8	Share
52	Growing Wild or Tame	Proverbs 29:15, 23–24	Discipline
54	Grow Protected	Proverbs 27:12; Daniel 12:1	Prepare
56	Enemies of Blackberries	Proverbs 26:2: Deuteronomy 28:1, 15	Obedience
58	Was It Worth It?	Revelation 5:12	Earth's Harvest
60	Appendix A: Tree of Life		
62	Appendix B: Tree of Good and Evil—The Tree of Hate		
64	Appendix C: Bibliography		
66	Appendix D: The Law of the Farm		

Introduction for Terry McComb book

In our modern world, science may seem to explain everything. Scientists have replaced priests and pastors as the authorities to whom people turn for answers to the ultimate questions. The problem is that the answers provided tend to hide profound religious biases, are often bizarre and science itself is built on a metaphysical foundation to which many scientists appear oblivious. We need Bible-believing pastors and theologians more than ever, especially when dealing with the big questions on every thinking person's mind. These include: Where did I come from? How should I live my life? What will happen to me after I die? As you read *The Gospel According to a Thornless Blackberry*, you will find plenty of reasons why Bible-believing pastors like Pr. Terry McComb are so vital to our understanding of nature and our appreciation of the natural world that God made to sustain us, to amaze us and to teach us about Him.

I still remember the first time I met Pr. McComb, you probably will too if this book is your first introduction to his thinking. Over the years I've been impressed by his talent for both pointing out the beauty that pervades the creation as well as lessons we can learn about our Creator from what we see. As Christians, we understand that our assurance of salvation is rooted in faith in what Jesus Christ has done for us. Just as we were created through grace and no merit of our own, we are saved through God's grace, but as the Apostle James wrote, "Faith without works is dead" (James 2:26). The natural response to realizing that our salvation is our Creator's gift is to ask what His purpose was in making and redeeming us. We find ourselves driven to learn God's will and strive to live according to it. This practical transformation in how Christians live is a focus of Pr. McComb's ministry and this book.

My hope is that in reading *The Gospel According to a Thornless Blackberry* you will enjoy and embrace the very practical life lessons Pr. McComb draws from the fascinating work of Luther Burbank. Burbank may not have been the perfect ideal, either as a scientist or in his religious beliefs (before dying, he actually called himself and "infidel"), but this illustrates why we look to Christ as our example rather than humans. In addition, it shows how the discoveries and methods of scientists are not something for Christians to fear. No matter what Burbank believed, the peach, plum, blackberry and other varieties he bred remain just as tasty. In the same way, everything that is discovered about nature, no matter who discovers it, reveals something about nature's Creator for those prepared to see and appreciate it.

If you are seeking to understand God's purpose in your life and to lead others to Him, but find yourself encumbered by "thorns" that compromise your happiness and your ministry, I suspect that your time with *The Gospel According to a Thornless Blackberry* will do what an encounter with our Creator always does. As occurred with those who sat at Jesus feet while he recounted parables based on the observation of nature, burdens will be shed, purpose will become clear, joy will grow and your ministry, through Christ's strength and the power of the Holy Spirit, will flourish. That's time well-spent!

Timothy G. Standish, PhD, Senior Scientist, Geoscience Research Institute

Preface

In the wonder world of nature God has placed the key to unlock the treasure house of His word. The *unseen is illustrated by the seen*. Divine wisdom, eternal truth and infinite grace are understood by the things God made.

It is a refreshing truth that the same laws that we find in the natural world are the same laws of the true God, the Creator.

The following pages will tell how Luther Burbank (1849–1926) removed thorns from the blackberry plant. The methods he used and the time involved make it a true nature mystery story, stranger than fiction. It also sheds clear light on a "thorny" portion of scripture such as Romans 6,7, and 8.

We recommend reading this story with a real blackberry bush nearby. Take one lesson at a time in the out-of-doors. Let the child feel real thorns and eat real blackberry fruit thus the character lessons may be reinforced and learned. It would be nice as you study this book to provide your children with a taste of fruit from a real thornless blackberry plant. Most of the fresh blackberries found in supermarkets, are the thornless variety.

It is our hope that in today's illustration from nature—from thorns to thornless—all can see how God transforms lives from selfishness to love, from the carnal nature to partaking of His divine nature.

Denominational churches have increased from ten in the 1800's to over 30,000 in 2017. The youth of today are puzzled to know where to find the true God. It is commonly taught in high schools and universities that there are many religious leaders, of whom Jesus is one, and that the Bible is one religious book among many. We believe the study of nature as seen today will reveal the Bible as the only true account of origins, and that Jesus was its Creator.

This book has been in the making for 30 years. A lifetime of careful observation of nature and scripture has found fruition on the following pages. The artist, Vera McMurdo, never lived to see this publication. How pleased she will be resurrection morning, to see an eternal harvest of boys and girls who took the "seeds" of truth from her pictures, and grew up to the mature, full stature of Jesus Christ. The authors hope to attract youth to a revelation of God as seen in His world of nature. Scripture always confirms genuine science. Genuine science often holds the key to unlock difficult passages of scripture such as Romans 5–8.

Briars and Thorns

One does not wander far in the wonder-world of nature before we become painfully aware that something is wrong. Why? Painful welts arise from pricks; rattlesnake's fangs inject poison; beautiful roses grow on thorny bushes; spiders kill flies; birds kill spiders; and man kills birds. Here nature needs an interpreter.

Genesis 3:17–18 tells us, *"Cursed is the ground for thy sake, thorns and thistles shall it bring forth to thee."* Because of man's rebellion against God's law of love, the rulership of this world became Satan's. In his laboratory, Satan began to twist everything that God made "very good." All the "badness" he developed is only spoiled goodness. In the thorns, fangs, and stingers, we see how Satan intends to establish a kingdom where each one views the other as an enemy to be conquered or destroyed. In the parable of the wheat and tares (weeds), He said, *"An enemy hath done this"* (Matthew 13:28).

The theory of evolution speculates that plants grew thorns because they needed extra protection. This would give blackberries incredible intelligence. They would recognize they have a problem and grow pointed barbs to solve it. That kind of wisdom is opposite to evolution's random chance or luck theory.

The Creator chose to come to this world to bear the curse of sin that was ours and in exchange give fallen man divinity that was His. When Burbank chose to take thorns out of blackberry bushes, he demonstrated the method Jesus used when He overcame evil with good.

PRACTICAL PROJECT

As a family take a nature hike and see how many briers, thorns or stingers, you can find. How does this show the working of an evil power against Jesus' love and peace? As a family, study how Bethlehem's cradle was God's answer to the problem of pain and evil. (Start with Luke 1:26–35.)

Briars and Thorns

Law of Genetics

Luther Burbank was a plant scientist in Sebastopol, California in 1880. Through selective plant development he produced many new species. One of his experimental projects was to develop thornless blackberries on his ten-acre farm.

To remove the thorns, he would have to remove one of the curses that came as a result of sin. "Thorns also and thistles shall it bring forth unto thee and thou shalt eat the herb of the field" (Genesis 3:18). The big question is; how would you remove one of the curses of sin from blackberries?

Burbank had a very simple understanding of what we call the law of genetics. Simply put, it means we reap what we sow. Galatians 6:7–9 explains, "Be not deceived; God is not mocked: For whatsoever a man soweth, that shall he also reap. For he that soweth to his flesh shall of the flesh reap corruption; but he that soweth to the Spirit shall of the Spirit reap life everlasting. And let us not be weary in well doing: for in due season we shall reap if we faint not." According to the law of genetics, you can't reap what you don't sow.

Burbank understood that if you cross one plant with another, the dominant characteristics will come through in the next generation. His idea was simple: if you cultivate what you want and get rid of what you don't want, eventually you will harvest what you want.

This idea is expressed in Romans 12:21, "Be not overcome of evil, but overcome evil with good." So, if you want to have a thornless blackberry, you plant and cultivate blackberries that have less thorns and eventually you can succeed in getting rid of the thorns altogether. This was Burbank's plan.

PRACTICAL PROJECT

Design the family tree for Dad and Mom. Place it on a poster and take them back four generations. Use pictures of relatives if you can find them. Look over your family tree to discover what are the strong characteristics in hair color, color of eyes, and height of individuals. What about temperaments? What about talents? Skills?

Law of Genetics

Cultivation

Luther Burbank brought the Wachusetts Thornless Blackberry from the eastern part of the United States. It was not truly thornless, but it had less thorns than other blackberries. On his farm he planted 1500 of these seedlings.

As these seedlings grew up, he looked them over carefully. Around the plants with less thorns he would tie a little white piece of cloth. Then he destroyed all the rest, keeping only those that had less thorns. Burbank's program for dealing with the thorns in blackberries was simple. *He cultivated the best and destroyed the rest.*

Here is a very important principle of Christian growth. He did not just cultivate the best, he *destroyed* the rest. That's what the word cultivation means: selectively letting one thing live, and letting everything else around it die. This is the principle that the Apostle Paul was trying to get across:

> That you put off, concerning your former conduct,
> the old man which grows corrupt according to the
> deceitful lusts, and be renewed in the spirit of your
> mind, and that you put on the new man which was
> created according to God, in true righteousness and holiness.
> (Ephesians 4:22–24)

> If you live according to the flesh, you will die; but if by the Spirit
> you put to death the deeds of the body, you will live.
> (Romans 8:13)

🌿 PRACTICAL PROJECT

In a garden, plant two short rows of radishes. In one row let the weeds grow with the radishes. In the next row let only the radishes grow, weeding it carefully. Note the differences. What difference would cultivation make in your spiritual life?

Cultivation

Culling Out

Burbank's garden was too small to allow anything to grow except what he needed. There could be no in-between. He removed all bushes with the most thorns because his goal was only thornless bushes.

We may think music, videos, or computer games are just entertainment, neither good or bad. We don't see the kind of person they eventually produce. Whatever comes into my senses, becomes a permanent part of me. We have access today to the tree of "good and evil" via the medias! Some music, DVDs, and games promote lawless "thorns" of killing, rape, lies, and stealing! These are tares planted by the enemy who Jesus said has done this. These tares are seeds that produce the fruits of the flesh found in Galatians 5:19–21.

Like Burbank's garden, our life is too short to have time to grow both good and evil! We must choose the good and true and uproot evil. God knows that if we listen to that music or watch that video they become "seeds" we will not want to reap as an adult.

With the sword of the spirit, the Bible, we can cut out the lawless 'thorns" from our internet. We can remove killing games, porno magazines, books, music, or DVDs that glorify sin. We can stop cheating at school. These evils are to be removed from our life as surely as Burbank's knife removed unwanted, thorny bushes from his garden.

"Likewise, you also, reckon yourselves to be dead indeed to sin, but alive to God in Jesus Christ our Lord... And do not present your members as instruments of unrighteousness to sin, but present yourselves to God as being alive from the dead, and your members as instruments of righteousness to God" (Romans 6:11, 13).

Sin must die in a way similar to the way Burbank removed unwanted thorny blackberry bushes. With his knife he cut out that bush. It lived no longer! It ceased to be part of his garden. God has one remedy for sin—death! Life ceases. If death is not the ceasing of life, then God can never remove sin from His universe garden. (See Romans 8:13.)

🌿 PRACTICAL PROJECT

In your radish garden, experiment which works better—to cut the weeds off with a knife at the top, or to pull them out by the roots? As a family, discuss how you would do that spiritually in the light of Romans 6:11–13.

Culling Out

13

Thornless Bushes... But Yucky Fruit

By the third generation of seed planting, Burbank had 1,500 seedlings which had no thorns! Impressively, the genetic law in plants and the Ten Commandment Law are in harmony! Exodus 20:5 tells us, *"The curse of sin reaches to the third and fourth generation..."*

Burbank had removed the thorns from blackberries. Wonderful! However, one small problem still remained. The fruit on those bushes was small, nubby, and tasteless! What good are thornless bushes with yucky fruit?

In a similar way, some people have succeeded in outwardly obeying the rules. They don't swear, smoke, drink, do drugs, or run around. Badness held in check is not righteousness, but rather bad goodness, for it can fool both the doer and onlooker. It is life-less! A dead person does not smoke, drink, do drugs, or run around either.

I can believe in Christ and have a great deal of knowledge about him, but unless I receive Jesus and actually surrender my will to His control, I will never bear His divine fruit. Jesus said: *"You will know them by their fruits"* (Matthew 7:16). God is looking for his divine fruit on thornless human bushes. It is not enough to stop swearing or hitting or hurting classmates or myself. We need His divine fruits of the Spirit (See Galatians 5:22, 23) to replace our carnal selfish fruits.

Baptism is a symbol not only of our death with Christ but also of our resurrection with His New Life (Romans 6:4). *"But yield yourselves onto God as those who are alive from the dead, and your members as instruments of righteousness to God"* (Romans 6:13).

What would Burbank now do to get good fruit?

🌿 PRACTICAL PROJECT

How can we as a family not only avoid harming our neighbors but how can we do them positive good? What can we do that would demonstrate the fruit of Divine love for them?

Thornless Bushes... But Yucky Fruit

Patient Cross-Breeding

Burbank was not discouraged after ten years of experiments, even though he still had thorns and yucky fruit. Year after year he labored on in hopeful expectancy. He could do this because he had a knowledge of two things: (1) he had plants that had the most desirable qualities; (2) he knew the law of genetics was sure and certain as sunrise.

The spiritual law of genetics is both good and bad news. Adam's sin was bad news to Adam and his children. Adam could give only what he had—a sinful nature. *"For as by one man's disobedience many were made sinners..."* (Romans 5:19).

This same law, which is our curse from Adam is also our hope in Christ: *"...so also by one Man's obedience many will be made righteous."* (Romans 5:19). This law gives us an assurance and *hope* that is certain, though at the moment we still have some thorns and yucky fruit. From the Creator's point of view, if you sow and cultivate His Seed, and destroy the rest, it is as if the full harvest had already happened. "*...you are complete in Him*" (Colossians 2:10).

In the same way, a Christian family can claim Bible promises with enthusiasm. *"For we were saved in this hope, but hope that is seen is not hope... But if we hope for what we do not see, we eagerly wait for it with perseverance"* (Romans 8:24, 25).

Hope is an excited expectancy! He, God, *"counts those things that are not as though they already were"* (Romans 4:17).

PRACTICAL PROJECT

When father and mother make a promise to their child, how much hope can the child put in that word? Is it as sure as the law of genetics? What about the word of the children? Can the parents put hope in it? In your little garden, how sure are you that you're going to reap a harvest of radishes? How long does it take? Do you have hope?

Patient Cross-Breeding

Spiritual Law of Genetics

Thorns produce thorns. Less thorns produce less thorns, until they are gone. This is the law Burbank followed.

The fruitage of this law produces the blessing of the fifth commandment.

Father A-1 is stubborn and selfish. By the "law of genetics" he will produce a stubborn selfish child.

Child A-2 reasons, "Why should I obey a selfish, stubborn father? I'm not going to do it! Now the child not only inherits but cultivates stubbornness. When he grows up and becomes a father, A-2 passes on the stubbornness of his father, plus his own, to his child, grandson A-3. Thus,"*You have done worse than your fathers*" Jeremiah 16:12. The fifth commandment of Exodus 20:12 reads, *"Honor thy father and mother that thy days may be long upon the land which the Lord thy God giveth thee."*

The Hebrew word used for honor in Exodus 20:12 is *"to be heavy."* The fifth commandment places children (and parents) under heavy responsibility to behave in an honorable manner; parents to the child and child to the parent.

On the opposite page, father A-1 is stubborn, therefore his child A-2 inherits stubbornness. This child breaks the fifth commandment, mocks his father's authority, and thus cultivates his father's weakness. When he grows up he is "a spitting image of his dad." The child of father A-2 is worse and the spiral is ever downward.

Father B-1 has the identical stubbornness of the first father, A-1, but in this case his child, B-2, by the grace of God, honors his father's position of authority.

To get along with a stubborn father, what character quality does this child develop? PATIENCE! This is the opposite quality of stubbornness. When he grows up and becomes a father, he has grace to cope with his own stubborn child. The grandchild inherits the grandfather's weakness plus his own father's good virtue. Thus, the seed quality is not as stubborn as was his forefather B-1.

The fifth commandment is God's answer to poor parenting. The "curse goes to third and fourth generations" (see Exodus 20:5, 6), but blessings are promised to 1000 generations.

PRACTICAL PROJECT

What specific family sins could we anticipate being a problem for children in your home? How could the principle of the fifth commandment counteract the effects of this sin?

Spiritual Law of Genetics

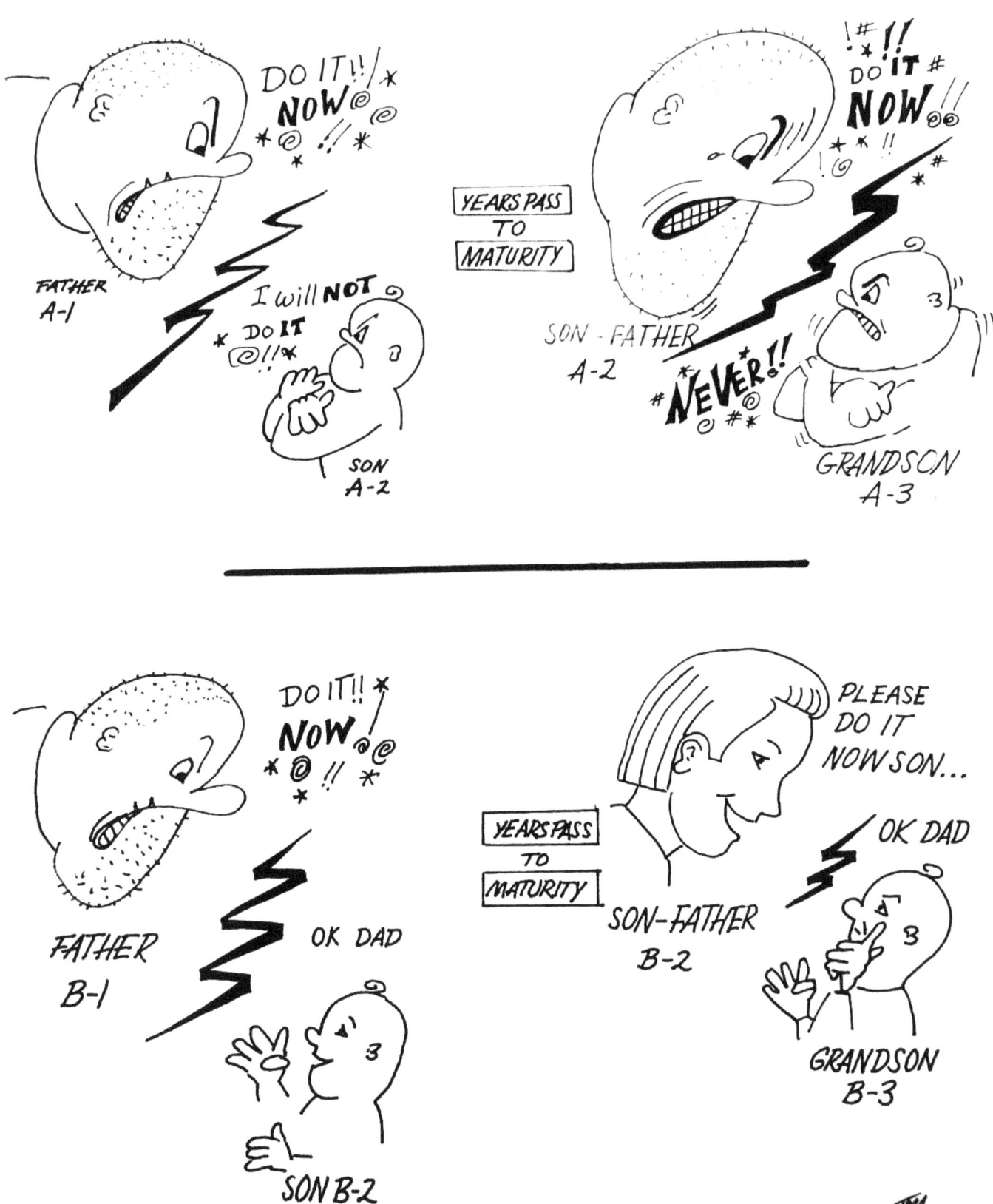

Stubborn Thorns

Year after year, Burbank planted generation after generation of blackberry seeds. During this process, Burbank discovered: "Every alternate generation of seeds produced only bushes with thorns. A characteristic in a plant which had existed for unknown generations is likely to be much more difficult to change." I call this Burbank's second law of genetics. The second generation produces only thorns.

In a similar way, when we are "born again" spiritually, we are surprised to discover more sins and sinful cravings than before. This may be the result of a second spiritual law of genetics. Paul said, *"But I see another law in my members, warring against the law of my mind, and bringing me into captivity to the law of sin which is in my members"* (Romans 7:23–25). The Creator must have had this law in mind when he commanded Israel in Deuteronomy 6:2, *"That thou teach thy children and thy children's children diligently, my law."*

The curse of sin (thorns) manifests itself in a more marked way every other generation in children as well as in blackberries. There is a social law which says that what parents allow in moderation the children will do in excess and the grandchildren will self-destruct. We need godly grandparents teaching and sharing God's law of love to their third generation. This is a challenge today. Grandparents often live far away from their grandchildren.

Burbank's second law of genetics (a crop of thorns) has no power of choice. We do! Let us choose life. *"I call heaven and earth as witnesses today against you, that I have set before you, life and death, blessing and cursing; therefore choose life, that both you and thy seed may live; that you may love the Lord your God, that you may obey His voice, and that you may cling to Him, for He is your life and the length of your days"* (Deuteronomy 30:19, 20). Israel failed in the third generation! In the end, Israel lost the promised land and reaped the promised curses of disobedience for 40 years.

PRACTICAL PROJECT

As a family, look at your family tree. What specific sins could we anticipate being a problem? How can you counteract the second law of genetics by cross-breeding in Scriptural texts which will counteract sin's baleful effects? How can grandparents bless their grandchildren at a distance?

Stubborn Thorns

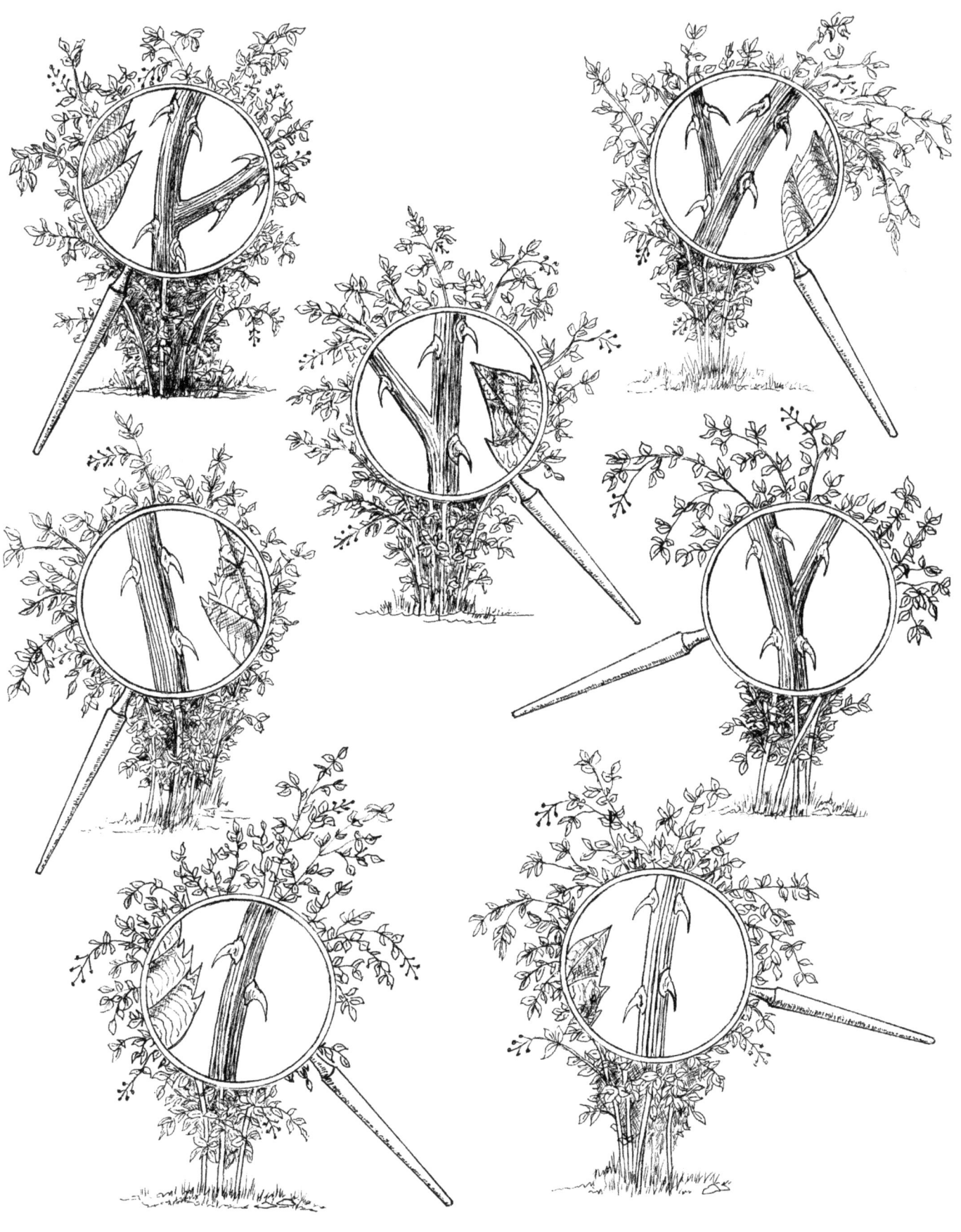

Seeds

The genius of Burbank lay in his skill to select seeds. He believed that if you plant what you want, in time you will reap what you sow. The secret of removal of thorns in blackberries lay in the seed.

Locked inside the tiny, brown seed, are submicroscopic DNA molecules. The seed of the blackberry (rosaceae), requires a period of time to sleep while the baby bit of life inside the seed matures, then springs into life.

In Holy Scripture we find the word "seed" referred to 250 times. In Mark 4:26, 27 we read, "And He said, 'The kingdom of God is as if a man should scatter seed on the ground, and should sleep by night and rise by day, and the seed should sprout and grow, he himself does not know how.'" The miracle of multiplication in seeds has been marveled at since they were first placed in the Garden of Eden on the third day of creation.

Paul refers to this fact in 2 Corinthians 9:10: "Now may He who supplies seed to the sower and bread for food, supply and multiply the seed you have sown and increase the fruits of your righteousness." Here the seed does not reproduce just one seed, but it multiplies!

In harmony with this great law of genetics it is for us to choose what we want to see *multiply* in our life. If we choose smiles and kindness they will multiply themselves. Sow a frown and a gripe and they also multiply. We are the sowers and reapers of our choices both in our own life as well as in the lives of our family and friends!

🌿 PRACTICAL PROJECT

Ask Mother to buy some blackberries at the store. Carefully count how many seeds there are in one berry. If you planted one seed and it grew a bush that produced 12 berries, how many seeds would you have at the end of the first year's growth? If you planted all of them and they all produced the same number of seeds as your first berry, how many seeds would you have at the end of year two? Now, if all these were planted, how many would you have at the end of year three? This explains how God feeds our hungry world by multiplying seeds!

Seeds

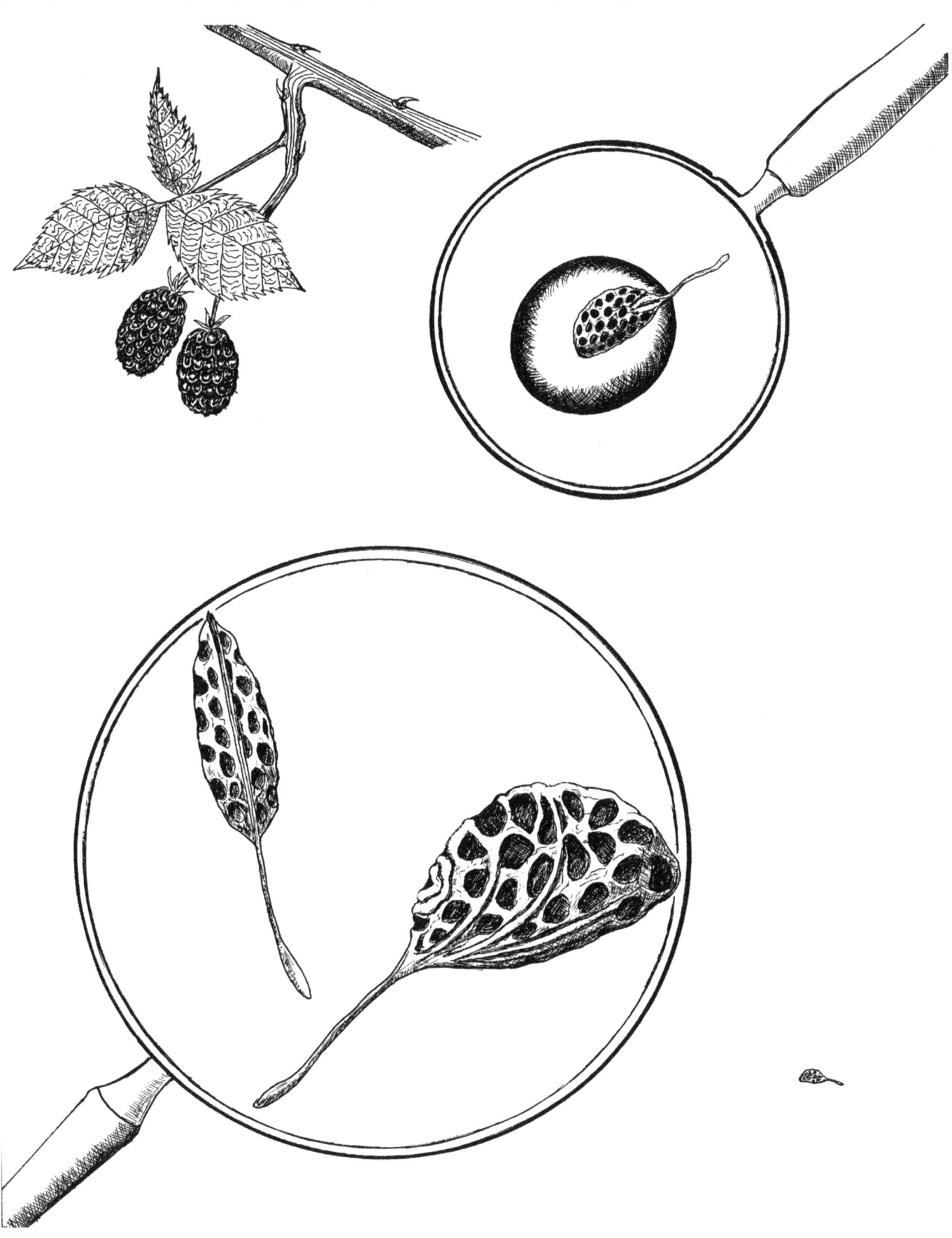

23

Clean Garden

Six miles east of Santa Rosa, is found the village of Sebastopol, California. Just west of this town is located the 10-acre research farm of Burbank. This small acreage left no room for trash or waste. Burbank kept a clean orchard. Near the western edge of his property he piled the day's cuttings and culls. This pile grew week by week until it was a stack about 20 feet long by six feet wide and equally as high. Once a year Burbank had his "$10,000 bonfire." That is what he figured it cost to collect. He burned these cast-offs so they would not contaminate new generations with their old ways. He wanted no piles of rotting vegetation to attract fungus, molds or disease.

In a similar way at the end of time, God will have a clean universe where sin and sinners are no more. Jesus refers to this time in the parable of the tares saying:

Therefore as the tares are gathered and burned in the fire, So shall it be at the end of this age. The Son of man will Gather out of His kingdom all things that offend, and those who practice lawlessness, and will cast them into the furnace of fire. (Matthew 13:40–42)

2 Peter 3 discusses the end of the wicked. Verse 7 tells us *"The heavens and earth which are now, will be burned up."* The same verse says it is not burning now but will burn after the judgment. Malachi 4:1–3 tells us the effect of the fire will leave neither root nor branch of wickedness: *"For they shall be ashes under the soles of your feet on the day I do this sayeth the Lord of Hosts."*

The effect of this fire is eternal in results. 2 Peter 3:13 says, after the smoke and fire, *"Nevertheless, we according to His promise, look for a new heaven and a new earth, in which righteousness dwells."*

🌿 PRACTICAL PROJECT

It is well to have a conscience clearing time, before bedtime, when we clear up family misunderstandings and sins of the day. *"Strive to have a conscience without offense towards God and man"* (Acts 24:16). Fathers can lead their families nightly to experience. 1John 1:9: *"If we confess our sins, He is faithful and just to forgive us our sins and to cleanse us from all unrighteousness."* Life is too short to be a sin collector! Each night we can send all our confessed sins on to judgment so we have a clean house and a clear conscience by the blood and mediation of Jesus.

Clean Garden

Slow Growth, Needs TIME

Burbank in hope followed an eight-step program on blackberries year after year. He simply cultivated the best and destroyed the rest. **First**, he carried pollen from one plant to another. This was done with several plants. Each was carefully marked and the crossings recorded. **Second,** he harvested seeds from these plants and cleaned them carefully keeping only the healthiest seeds. **Third,** he planted these seeds in shallow boxes called flats. **Fourth**, he watched each plant in the flats the moment they poked above the surface. **Fifth,** when a plant revealed undesirable qualities it was destroyed. **Sixth**, after all were eliminated except those which showed no fault, the remaining plants were transplanted into test beds where they had more room and were given the best of care. Every day, he examined each bed. **Seventh,** if any weakness could be found, in the newly transplanted plant it was removed. Daily, the number of plants in the experiment decreased. **Eighth,** the best of these plants were again crossed and recorded and he started the whole process of eight steps all over again! Often, he might use millions of plants for each experiment. He exercised "hope" in his daily labor.

Paul in Romans 5:2–5 said, "Rejoice in hope of the glory of God. And not only that, but we also glory in tribulations, knowing that tribulation produces perseverance; and perseverance, character; and character, hope." The same genetic law which is our doom in the first Adam, is our hope in the Second Adam! Same law-but different seeds!!

"Abraham waited 100 years for Isaac the son of promise, "Who, contrary to hope, in hope believed… He did not waver at the promise of God through unbelief, but was strengthened in faith, giving glory to God, and being fully convinced that what He had promised He was also able to perform" (Romans 4:18, 20).

PRACTICAL PROJECT

See the end from the beginning. Have a 5-year family planning night.

Where and what shall we hope to be doing then? What seeds shall we plant as a family working toward these goals? It is the same act of the mind to believe or not believe. What do we put our "faith" in?

Slow Growth, Needs TIME

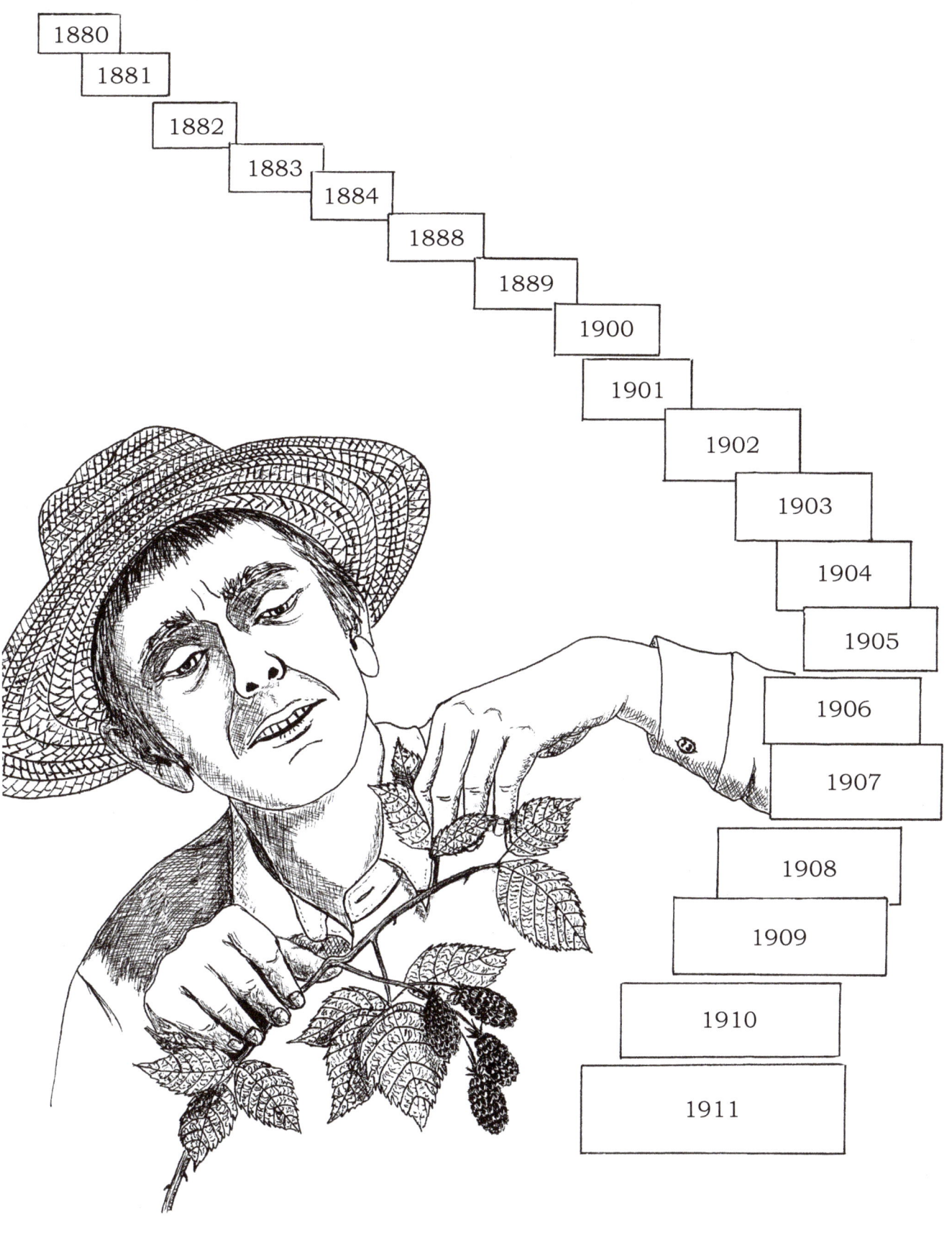

Slow Growth Wait

Burbank faced every morning with hope! His hope was the certainty of the law of genetics, and in ability to select right seeds. Hope is an excited expectancy of what *will* happen just as if it had already happened. We need hope in the Christian life. Romans 7:21 says, "I find then a law, that evil is present with me, the one who wills to do good. For I delight in the law of God according to the inward man. But I see another law in my members, warring against the law of my mind." This law of sin which is in the body, is the old genetic law of sin that dates back to Adam.

The Holy Spirit creates enmity or a genetic war between these two natures. "O wretched man that I am! Who will deliver me from this body of death? I thank God—through Jesus Christ our Lord! So then, with the mind I myself serve the [genetic] law of God, but with the flesh the [genetic] law of sin" (Romans 7:24, 25).

This old genetic sin nature of Adam still produces thorns now and then, but we are to cultivate the divine seed of Jesus Christ and execute the old thorns still hanging around. Theologians call this process sanctification which is the work of a lifetime.

Like Burbank, we cultivate the seed of Jesus and execute by the "Spirit" the thorns of the flesh. See Romans 8:13.

Hebrews 11:1 says, "Now faith is the substance of things hoped for, the evidence of things not seen." "For we are saved in this hope. But hope that is seen is not hope; for why does one still hope for what he sees. But if we hope for what we do not see, we eagerly wait for it with perseverance" (Romans 8: 24, 25).

PRACTICAL PROJECT

Put a mark behind the kitchen door as to how tall you are. Every month measure yourself and see how much you grow. Look at mother and dad. How tall are they? Rest contentedly in hope that you too one day will be as tall as they. As a family, memorize 2 Corinthians 4:16–18.

Slow Growth Wait

Full Fruit on Thornless Bushes

In the year 1911, after 30 years of labor, Burbank came rushing in to his office. "Just taste this," he said. In his hand were large, luscious, juicy, sweet blackberries. They had grown on bushes totally without thorns. Well might Burbank rejoice. The years of patient labor were finally rewarded.

Blackberries must be fully ripe before picked. One cannot go by their shiny blackness. Appearance is not enough. When fully ripe blackberries lose their shininess and become slightly dull then they are ready to be picked and eaten.

A sinner never boasts about being thornless, for he knows about the thorns held in check by the grace of the Lord Jesus. "God forbid that I should boast except in the cross of our Lord Jesus Christ, by whom the world has been crucified to me and I to the world" (Galatians 6:14).

Full fruits of the spirit on thornless human nature. Is this possible? The Lord Jesus has been working experiments of grace on the human heart whose results are truly amazing. Revelation 14:4, 5 describes these people, "These were redeemed from among men, being firstfruits to God and to the Lamb. And in their mouth was found no deceit, for they are without fault before the throne of God."

Burbank only needed to cross breed one thorny bush into his thornless bushes and all their children would be thorny. So it is with the sanctified Christian. *"Those who belong to Christ Jesus have nailed their sinful nature to his cross and crucified them there. Since we are living by the Spirit, let us follow the Spirit's leading in every part of our live"* (Galatians 5:24, 25). The fruits of the Spirit will make any home a little bit of Heaven on earth. *"You will always harvest what you plant"* (Galatians 6:7).

PRACTICAL APPLICATION

Matthew 7:16, 17, 20 says, "You will know them [false prophets] by their fruits. Even so, every good tree bears good fruit, but a bad tree bears bad fruit." How can we as a family practice experiments of love on each other so love can grow visible fruit in each member's life? One way would be to study each other's happiness.

Full Fruit on Thornless Bushes

Plant Timing

The Blackberry plant has a flowering stage in its life cycle. The flower parts are five white petals and, in their center, multiple pistils, which are the female parts. This blossom is very similar to a strawberry blossom. Both strawberries and blackberries are an aggregate fruit. Aggregate fruits form from one flower that has several female pistils. Each pistil will develop a new seed.

The picture on the opposite page illustrates that one can have a flower and fruit at the same time. But flowers always grow before fruit. The gradual development of fruit requires patience, proper nutrition, sunshine and water.

In a similar way, a person cannot be a baby, child, youth, adult, and old person all at the same time. Ecclesiastes 3:1 reveals: *"To everything there is a season, a time for every purpose under heaven."* Jesus invites us: *"Therefore you shall be perfect, just as your Father in heaven is perfect"* (Matthew 5:48).

The question is, when are plants or people perfect? As an infant, a child, adult, or a grandparent? The good news is that at each stage of growth, as its needs are met, we may be perfectly surrendered to the will of our Creator. At the flower stage there is perfection of blossoms, but blackberries are famous, not for flowers, but for their fruit. At each stage, as Christians, we are to be perfectly conformed to the will of our Maker.

A baby has a relationship to its mother, so does the toddler, the school-aged child, and teenager. As a child's self-control and self-government increase, the mother's responsibility and caretaking decrease and relationships with other authorities increase.

Time creates change. These changes can create insecurity, fear, or conflict. In the blackberry, each stage has its own special beauty, dangers, and function. These changes are silent, slow, and minute, but certain. The stem nourishes all four stages of this growth. Galatians 6:9 encourages us: *"And let us not grow weary while doing good, for in due season we shall reap if we do not lose heart."*

PRACTICAL PROJECT

All children seek freedom. Freedom increases as we demonstrate self-control by faithfully doing our chores: clean our room, make the bed, do dishes, etc. Doing our chores means doing them on time, with excellence, and without complaining or being reminded. As we exercise self-control by being responsible to fulfill our chores, we earn trust and more freedom. These changes take time.

Plant Timing

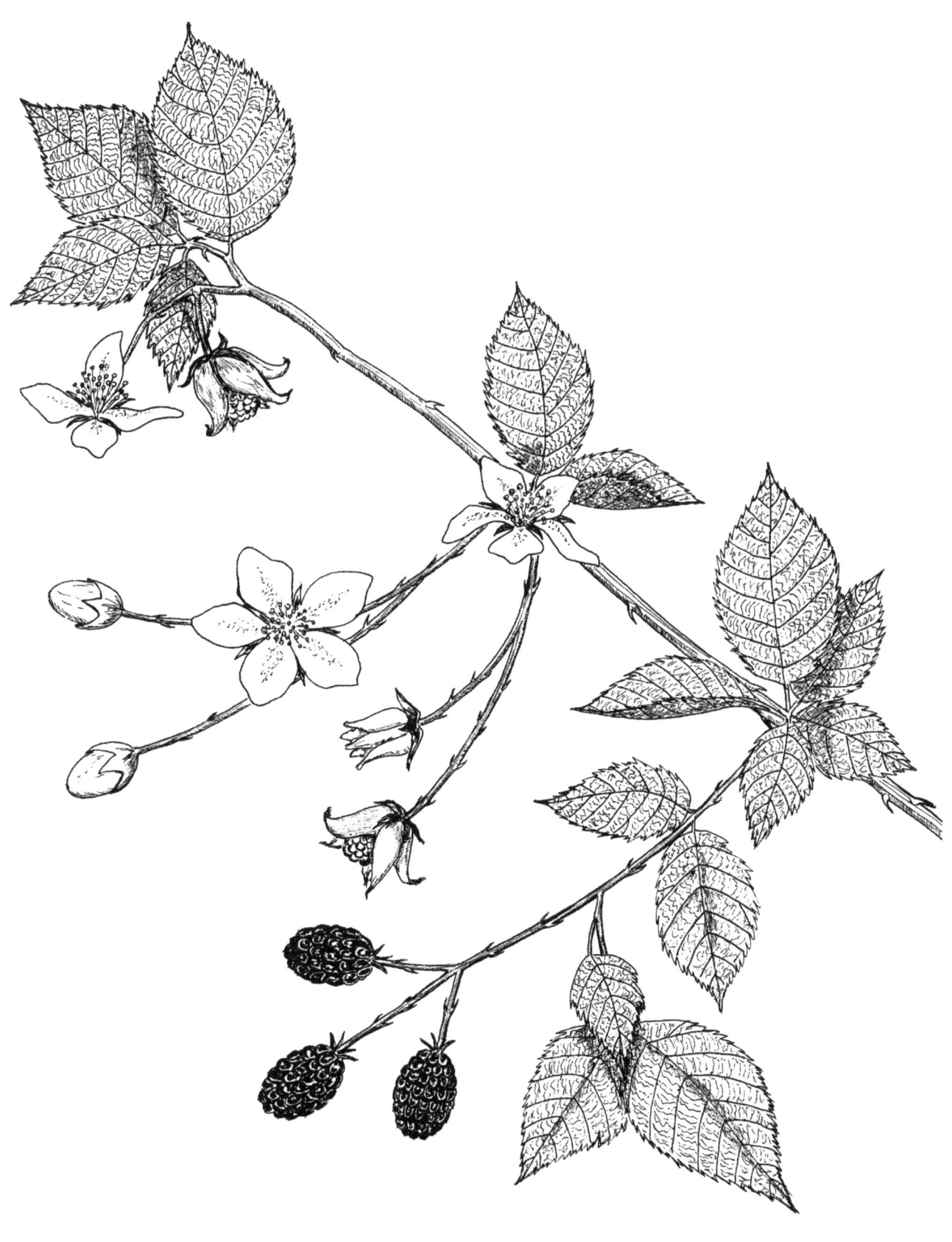

Delicious Fruit on Thornless Bushes

Luther Burbank had demonstrated the law of the farm— "we reap what we sow." By cultivating the best and destroying the rest, he finally reaped full delicious fruit on bushes that had no thorns. He had worked the law of genetics backwards to Genesis 1, where all of God's original plants had wonderful fruit and no thorns to mar their beauty. This foundational law, created on the third day of creation, is a major law of life. It operates in plants, animals, birds and in our own human bodies. It also operates mentally and spiritually in our minds.

Burbank used only God's invisible law of genetics to remove the curse of sin (thorns), and it required 30 years of time to do so. This is almost one lifetime. Think what Jesus can do using the same invisible law of genetics to remove the curse of sin and restore back the image of God in our human, mortal mind! By cultivating the divine promises of Scripture we can become partakers of His divine nature. 2 Peter 1:4 promises, "God has given us exceeding great and precious promises, whereby we become partakers of the divine nature and escape the corruption that is in the world through lusts."

In other words, if we cultivate the divine, sinless human nature of the "seed of the woman", Jesus Christ, and by the Holy Spirit "mortify" (kill) the thorns (deeds of our fallen nature), we will reap all the sinless fruits of the Spirit in our lives now! Full divine fruit on our human nature. We can vindicate the law of love by "abiding in Christ." Christ's divine, sinless nature, which becomes mine through faith, is immeasurably greater than the thorns in my old, sinful nature. Paul summarized this great truth in the last promise of Romans 8:37: "In (abiding in) Christ we are more than conquerors..." His divine powers indwelling in us is immeasurably greater than our degenerate, sinful, fallen nature. It is like killing mosquitos with an atomic bomb! Prayerfully consider the Tree of Love versus the Tree of Hate found on the closing pages of this book.

PRACTICAL PROJECT

As a family, examine all the media that enters your home: TV, DVDs, internet, computer games, music, books, and magazines. Ask yourselves: Do any of them carry "thorns" of the sin nature? Do they carry the DNA of the fruits of the Spirit? How safe is our home from the invisible "virus" of sin? How can we unitedly write God's Law of Love on the door posts of our house?

Delicious Fruit on Thornless Bushes

All blackberries that you buy at the market come from thornless plants. Every time you buy them, you can thank Luther Burbank for his 30 years of work.

First Fruit Love

As Burbank popped the large, flavor-filled Blackberries in his mouth, picked from totally thornless bushes, he savored their awesome flavor. Blackberry taste is so uniquely delicious, unlike any other berry.

"Taste and see that the Lord is good" (Psalm 34:8). Love is the first fruit of the Spirit to grow on thornless human bushes. The Bible states the origin of human life as: "Then God said, 'Let us make human beings in our image to be like us...so God created human beings in His own image. In the image of God He created them; male and female He created them" (Genesis 1:26, 27, NLT). In love God created Adam to love Eve and she loved him and they loved God. This very first relationship was selfless love. "The constant flow of human affection is the most delightful of all human sensations. When fixed upon an object truly worthy of it and this flowing is not impeded or held back by any conflicting or counteracting influence, it is a source of happiness inexhaustible. Love desires the good or honor of its object not its own" (E.G. Marsh)*.

In other words, the principle of love is 100% totally selfless and focused on the happiness of the object of its affection. "This is real love, not that we love God, but that He loved us and sent His Son as a sacrifice to take away our sins" (1 John 4:10). "We love Him because He loved us first" (1 John 4:19). Selfless love must first come from outside ourselves, for a "me first" selfish heart cannot create it.

This love is the source for all the other fruits of the Spirit. Look at the tree of love. Jesus said, "You must love the Lord your God with all your heart, all your soul and all your mind. Love your neighbor as yourself. The entire law and all the demands of the prophets are based on these two commandments" (Matthew 22:37–40, NLT). This law was spoken and written by God's finger on two tablets of stone, front and back (Exodus 32:15). So God's law can be divided into four sections. Front of tablet one is how God wishes to be loved and without images or idols. Backside of tablet one, how we relate to God, reverence His name and no work on His seventh day, Saturday, to keep it holy. On the front of tablet two, the three commands are all about life. Life from our honorable parents, right for this life to continue, and right to procreate life, one man and one woman. Back side of tablet two is how to live this life with the right of ownership (not stealing), the right to truth or reality, and right to be thankful and not covet. All the fruits of the Spirit grow out from these 10 laws of love. Love is the fulfilling of this law.

PRACTICAL PROJECT

Write a love letter to each member of the family including both sets of grandparents.

---

*Edward Garrard Marsh, in 1847, delivered a series of 8 sermons, entitled "The Christian Doctrine of Sanctification."
This was part of the Bampton lecture at the University of Oxford.
On page 13 is found the love quote I use here.
It was later published as a book by the title, *The Christian Doctrine of Sanctification*.

First Fruit Love

Love and Joy

The fun part of blackberries is tasting them. Its sweet succulent taste makes it worthwhile.

The same is true of the spirit. The whole purpose of redemption is to restore God's Love (His image) in fallen man. 1 John 4:10 says, *"this is love . . . not that we loved God, but that He loved us and sent His Son to be the propitiation (atonement) for our sin."* Paul writes in Galatians 5:22, 23, *"But the fruit of the Spirit is love, joy, peace, longsuffering, kindness, goodness, faithfulness, gentleness, self-control."* "Therefore by their fruits you will know them" (Matthew 7:20).

A blackberry is a composite fruit with many seeds in one fruit. So with the fruit of His love. If we cultivate the seed of His love, all other fruits of the Spirit will be seen in our life. Jude 24 says, "Keep yourselves in the love of God, looking for the mercy of our Lord Jesus Christ unto eternal life." Those who fail to grasp his "Seed" will find themselves yielding to the dark negative natural seeds planted by Satan. Fruits are an unerring evidence of the seed we cultivate. Remember, Burbank got rid of thorns (the evidence of sin in three generations) but it took thirty years to get full fruit on thornless bushes. John 15:5 says, "He that abideth in me, and I in him, the same bringeth forth much fruit: for without me ye can do nothing." "By this My Father is glorified, that you bear much fruit" (John 15:8).

The first fruit of the Spirit is love. This is demonstrated by the way father treats mother, and mother treats father. This love relationship creates children. The way parents share love with their children and children with their parents is the first fruit they taste—love. Love creates the second fruit of the spirit—joy. The human heart delights in the joy of being loved unconditionally. Loved, not for what we do, but for who we are. Jesus said, "These things I have spoken to you, that My joy may remain in you, and that your joy may be full" (John 15:1). "Jesus, who for the joy that was set before him, endured the cross" (Hebrews 12:2). Jesus invites, "Enter into the joy of the Lord" (Matthew 25:21).

PRACTICAL PROJECT

Write a love note to each member of your family. Express to each what they mean to you. See if it creates JOY.

Love and Joy

39

Peace and Patience

When walking in nature away from the rush and noise of the city, we are awed by its peace. When we observe blackberry bushes in the garden or wild, there is a peace surrounding the plant.

When we have done wrong however, we experience the opposite. A war of guilt and fear rages. We have no rest. The storm continues until we follow 1 John 1:9 and confess the wrong, whether it is to our brother or sister, Mom or Dad, teacher or friend. Then we experience what David talks about in this text: "Great peace have those who love your law, and nothing causes them to stumble" (Psalm 119:165).

When we receive God's forgiveness and extend that same forgiveness to those who wrong us, it is like a shelter. It can be compared to a sweet, peaceful sleep, in a warm, snuggly bed while outside a storm is raging. Many try to still this storm of guilt and fear because they have an evil heart of unbelief and will not accept Jesus' death as a substitute for their sin.

Our story in *The Gospel According to a Thornless Blackberry* demonstrates the fruit of longsuffering—patient endurance. The effort, energy and sacrifice Mr. Burbank put forth to develop full fruit on thornless bushes is a marvel of longsuffering. He quietly worked year after year trusting the law of genetics, to cultivate the best and destroy the rest.

In a similar way, Jesus patiently waits for His children on earth to accept His love so that He could motivate them to pass on His love instead of selfishness. We shall never know until eternity the agony He endured waiting patiently for our acceptance of his love. What joy it must bring to His heart when we accept His love unconditionally and demonstrate the same tolerance, and longsuffering endurance when people wrong us and we tell them they are forgiven. What fragrant fruit this is in our homes. 1 John 4:11 says, "If God so loved us, we also ought to love one another."

Blackberry fruit is an aggregate fruit. In each little black ball is a separate seed, yet all the seeds all grow together to make one blackberry. Love joy, peace, and endurance—all these spiritual fruits grow together. Jesus gave this promise in John 16:33 concerning peace: "These things I have spoken to you that in Me you may have peace. In the world you will have tribulation, but be of good cheer, I have overcome the world."

PRACTICAL PROJECT

Our peace does not rest in ourselves, circumstances, or others. It rests unshakably in Jesus's victory over sin. How have you experienced this peace in the midst of a storm caused by people, circumstances, or things? Going to school is a practice of endurance. Did you demonstrate endurance on your most difficult assignment today?

Peace and Patience

Gentle Kindness and Goodness

When we plant a delicate plant as seed, do we plant it with gentleness or a rough, careless heart? Burbank transferred pollen from a flower of flavor to a bush with thorns with careful gentleness. He was doing the useful work of an insect or bee.

He learned to administer direction without impatience or anger. It's taking time to build a friendship along with correction. It's not just getting a job done, but doing it with gentle kindness. When Jesus corrected the "woman in adultery," he did so in a kind, gentle way that won her heart to purity. "For His merciful kindness is great towards us; and the truth of the Lord endureth forever" (Psalm 117:2). Those we correct with kindness should walk away motivated by our kindness to go in the direction we shared.

Burbank took thorns out of blackberries by cultivating only the "best." In this kind way he took the thorny plant all the way back to Genesis 1—full delicious fruit on plants with no thorns. The work of his life was deliciously good! Not only does it taste good, it is good for you. It's a natural dessert which enables one to build a strong healthy body.

That leads to the character quality called goodness. The Holy Spirit does good and only good. When He becomes our motivator we too can relate to one another in a way that's good and beneficial. Children find ways of doing good to their pets. It is the fruit that shows to the world that Jesus really lives. "Look how they love one another. Look how they treat each other." They don't take advantage of one another. In a selfish world, unselfishness is a rare taste treat. *"The earth is full of the goodness of the Lord"* (Psalm 33:5). *"O that men would praise the Lord for His goodness and for His wonderful works to the children of man"* (Psalm 107:15). No one can argue with goodness.

🌿 PRACTICAL PROJECT

Brotherly kindness is based on the theme of co-operation. It is the opposite of competition. As a family, play a game of ball with the aim of making the person up to bat a winner.

When God completed Creation in Genesis 1:31, we read: *"Then God saw everything that He had made, and indeed it was very good."* God does good and only good. As a family take sheet of paper and list how Dad does good for Mom and children. Then list how Mom does good to Dad and children. Then list how children do good to Mom and Dad and to each other. Goodness is a fun fruit of God's Spirit.

Gentle Kindness and Goodness

Faith and Gentle Meekness

Burbank's trust in God's invisible law of genetics enabled him to develop 234 new varieties using more than 46 different kinds of plants. His faith in this law enabled him to enthusiastically face every new day while doing his blackberry project for 30 years. God created this law: "after its kind"—the law of genetics. It's this foundational principle manifested in green that makes all life possible on planet earth.

Likewise, we, by faith, develop an unshakable trust in God's Word. Here He reveals the Ten Commandment law of love as the foundational principle that governs His unlimited universe. This law guarantees six personal rights that are found in the last six commandments regarding human relationships. These six "rights" could be called love for one another.

We feel anger when one of these six rights are violated. Gentle meekness is the ability to endure injury with patience and without resentment. Jesus demonstrated this gentleness when every "right" was stripped from Him on the cross. By faith Jesus continued to trust His heavenly Father when He paid the penalty for our sins—death. It is learning to have personal trust in the finished work by Christ on our behalf. Gentleness is so needed when we stay within the limits of love called "rights." When we do this, we preserve not only our own rights but also the rights of others.

PRACTICAL PROJECT

When one of our rights was violated today, did we respond with gentleness or anger? As a family, study Romans 12:14–21 and discuss how we can overcome evil with Christ's meekness, making His gentleness our own.

Meekness is the exact opposite of anger. When you trace anger to its roots you find a violation of rights. Every child and adult has six rights. They are clearly spelled out in the last six of the Ten Commandments which tell us how to love to one another.

Each tiny blackberry fruitlet hooks onto the stem. Each has a right to nourishment, strength, and protection. God in His infinite wisdom set limits to each little fruitlet. Each stays within its limit, thus preserving the right of each fruitlet.

If anger is a problem in your family, discuss which of the six rights were violated?

Who violated the "right" and when? Is there a pattern in time and space? When one of our rights are violated, what can we do to keep from becoming angry? Ownership is learned by owning toys, clothes, things, money allowances, etc. Only when we own something first, can we share, and sharing must be voluntary from the heart.

Faith and Gentle Meekness

45

Self-Control

The Blackberry fruit slowly ripens to maturity. It requires time and energy, both human and divine. The last fruit of the spirit to mature is called temperance, or self-control. Scripture says, "grow in the grace and knowledge of our Lord and Savior" (2 Peter 3:18).

There is no stopping place in the capacity to grow. When Adam and Eve ate the forbidden fruit, transgressing God's law of love, they acknowledged the serpent's authority as higher than God's. Man lost his self-control and came under the control of a demonic power. Every child of Adam since is born without self-control. He can only gain it back by accepting Jesus's love and direction for his life.

It is the great object of parents to implant self-control in their children so that when they leave home the fruit of self-control is mature. Self-control; not parent control, not peer control. Not controlled by circumstances or things. The child has learned how much Jesus loves and cares for them. They can say no to evil because they have learned how to say "yes" to Jesus. With that knowledge in place, our children are safe in this suffering world even though sometimes bad things may happen to us. We are safe to be trusted in God's eternal world because every action will be prompted by the eternal love of God in them.

PRACTICAL PROJECT

2 Peter 1:5–7 lists eight qualities: faith, virtue, knowledge, self-control, perseverance, goodness, brotherly kindness, and love. "For if these things are yours and abound, you will be neither barren nor unfruitful in the knowledge of our Lord Jesus Christ" (1 Peter 1:8).

The fruits of the Spirit are listed from faith to virtue, to knowledge, to self-control, to perseverance, to godliness, to brotherly kindness, to love. Why do you think the virtues listed are in a different order than Galatians 6:22? Paul is looking at the fruits from the Spirit's perspective. In 2 Peter we are looking at the fruits of the Spirit from a human perspective, but the fruits are the same.

As a family, discuss what you could do when tempted by your friends to lose self-control and turn control over to someone else, something else, or to a drug or drink, or to a feeling. What wording could you use that would be a firm "no" to the temptation and at the same time not a rejection of your friend? Suggestion: "I have set aside my body to be a dwelling place for the Holy Spirit. I want Him to control my thoughts, my words, my deeds, and actions. If I partake of this substance, I would be surrendering my control to a chemical. "Would you like to watch a video that shows how these chemicals could rob you of self-control?" Then thank them for their invitation.

Discuss other situations that call for self-control like eating or sexual desire. Battles are thought out before they are fought out!

Self-Control

Pruning

Blackberry vines are like all vines; they have to be pruned. Vines keep growing until they are useless. It is the same with human nature. Jesus said in John 15:5, "I am the vine ye are the branches: he that abides in Me and I in him, the same brings forth much fruit." "My Father is the husbandman…and every branch that beareth fruit, he purgeth it, that it may bring forth more fruit" (John 15:1). He loves us too much to let our selfish natures grow out of control. And where does this pruner work? In any area that grows beyond the six sides, or six limits, of love as are found in the last six of the Ten Commandments.

Having this truth in mind, let us by faith gladly learn to accept the reproofs of life. Then we will not dread or avoid them, but welcome them as friends.

He trims back our selfish growth. While we give up what we think we love, in the end we reap what we really do love: the loving character of God. "Humble yourself in the sight of the Lord and He will lift you up" (James 4:10). He never takes away one thing that if we could see from His perspective, we would not gladly part with. "All scripture is given by inspiration of God and is profitable for doctrine, *for reproof, for correction* [emphasis added], for instruction in righteousness that the man of God may be perfect, thoroughly furnished unto all good works" (2 Timothy 3:16,17).

PRACTICAL PROJECT

If we can learn to love reproof, there is no end to what we can learn. As a student, my teacher reproved my writing assignment. By heeding his reproof and corrections, he made a winner out of me, making my project a winner three years straight! The reproofs of his corrections were not pleasant, but winning was!

As a family, share when you suffered a great loss and in the end it turned out a blessing. Keep a record of these in your family record scrap book. Live your life with the end in mind. What do you want the harvest of life to be? God "declares the end from the beginning" (Isaiah 46:10). We need this same Wisdom in order to love reproof. If we can't handle reproof, school just ended for us. We are now going to learn the hard way. *"The way of the transgressors is hard"* (Proverbs 13:15).

Pruning

Where Blackberries Grow Best

Different types of blackberries will grow in different climates, but they do best in a carefully selected environment.

Most any type of soil will do, if drainage is good on the surface and in the soil. Plants can be harmed in any season of the year if water stands around the roots. Wet land is quite unsuitable as in such soil plants suffer from both cold and heat. The best soil is a deep mellow clay loom, well filled with humus.

Blackberry plants require plenty of moisture while the berries are growing and ripening. The amount of water needed is roughly the equivalent of one inch of rainfall per week. Irrigate enough to meet this requirement.

You and I have needs like the blackberry. We need spiritual water to grow, especially when we want to bear the fruits of the Spirit. If we take in more spiritual food than we utilize, even that spiritual food could be harmful to us, if we hear and don't do. "Be ye doers of the word, and not hearers only, deceiving your own selves" (James 1:22). In this way, the creative power that is in the word of God can vitalize our lives from the inside out. Then we can be a blessing to those we serve, at home first, then at school, or Church, or on the playground, or at our place of employment.

God has a message of hope "for them that dwell on the earth, and to every nation, and kindred, and tongue, and people" (Revelation 14:6). Go to BibleInfo.com to learn more about this last message of hope. Everyone needs this Hope.

🌿 PRACTICAL PROJECT

Buy a thornless blackberry plant from a nursery. Plant it in a deep mellow clay loam, filled with humus, and tend to its needs. Nurture your plant until it bears fruit. In the Parable of the Sower of Luke 8:5–15, the seed was the same, the sower was the same. The difference was the four kinds of soils. Blackberries cannot choose the kind of soil they would have. They are totally dependent on man, the caretaker, as to the kind of soil they are planted in and the kind of care they receive. Keep a record of the lessons you learn from this project of caring for a real thornless blackberry plant.

Where Blackberries Grow Best

51

Growing Wild or Tame

Blackberries are grown commercially in New York, as well as the Willamette Valley of Oregon, parts of California, Arkansas, Michigan, and other places. The plants do best when set in rows seven to nine feet apart, depending on the soil, and from three to four feet apart in each row. There should be room enough in order to carefully cultivate the land or top soil around them, being careful not to get too close to the shallow root system of the plant.

They do grow wild, particularly along the northwest coast of Washington, Oregon, and the coast of British Columbia. Here they are almost a pest growing wild with large vicious thorns. They grow in patches often 24 feet or more in size. To try and pick berries here is to get very deep cuts and lose our own blood!

In a similar way, we as people can grow wild, or lawless, living by feelings, self-centered, doing whatever feels good or comes naturally. Proverbs 29:15 says, "The rod and rebuke gives wisdom, but a child left to himself brings shame to his mother." We all have a fallen nature that needs to be denied and a need for unselfish love that must be developed. This love must come from outside our self, for a natural selfish heart cannot produce this. Luke 9:23, 24 says, "If anyone desires to come after Me, let him deny himself, and take up his cross daily, and follow Me. For whoever desires to save his life will lose it, but whoever loses his life for My sake will save it."

Like the blackberries, we need enough space (the space we need is TIME), so that we hear the voice of Jesus speaking to us every day from His Word and in prayer. If we receive His promises into our heart we will grow thereby.

PRACTICAL PROJECT

Note what grows naturally around your home and what grows under the taming care of man, like in a park. Notice what grows wild and that which is growing under cultivation. On the playground do you like to play with a selfish, angry, untrained boy or girl, or one who is respectful, courteous, and loving? Which kind of a playmate shall you be?

As a family, plan your lifestyle so each member has quiet time. When alone, we can fellowship with Jesus via His Word and private prayer.

Growing Wild or Tame

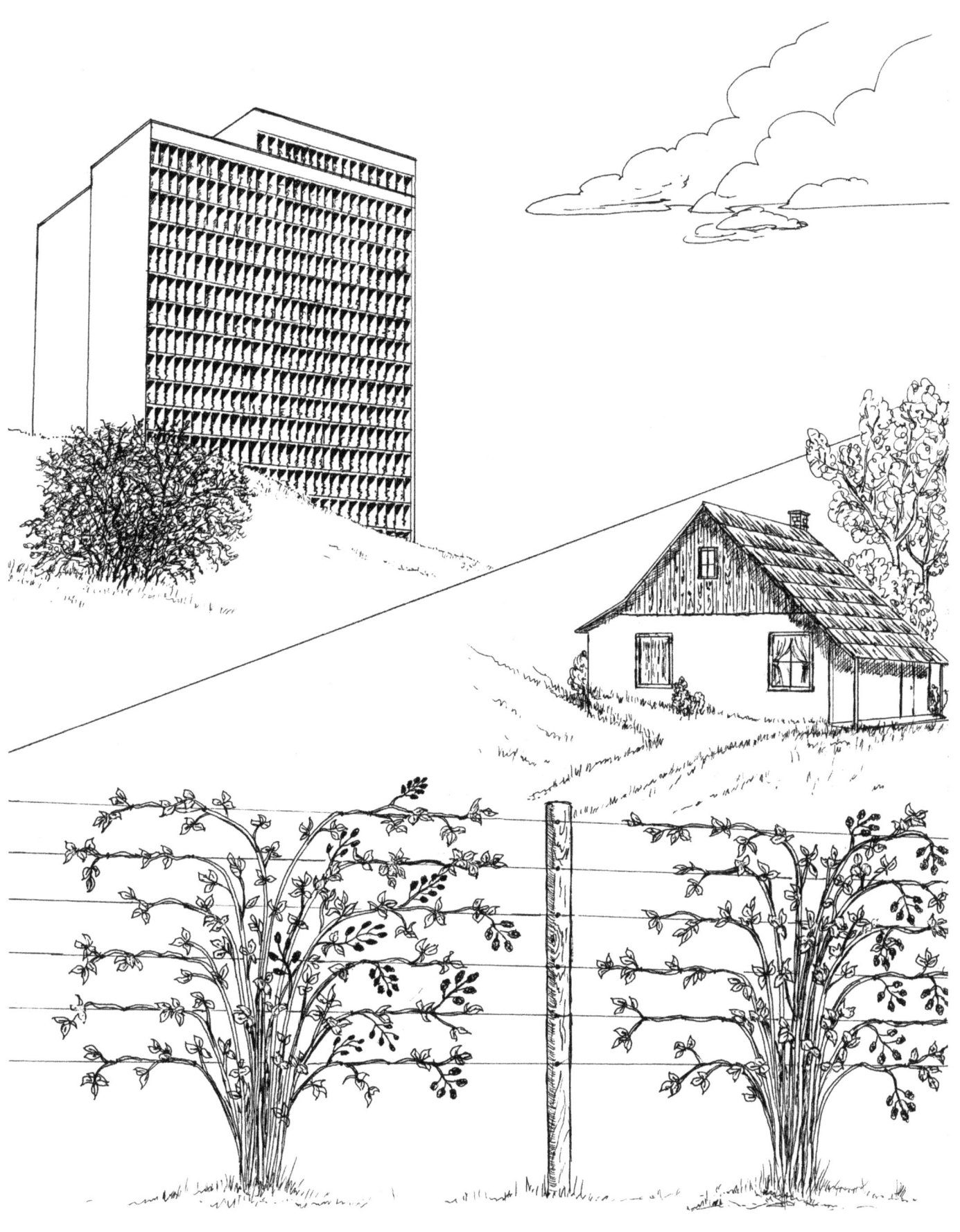

Grow Protected

If the temperature in winter drops below 10° F, blackberries need protection to survive and grow well. This protection will involve work, careful thought.

Step one. Cultivate land one month before freezing weather. **Step two.** Plant a cover crop of clover in August to supply humus and plant food necessary for blackberry.

Step three. When the canes become dormant before severe weather these need to be laid down and covered with mulch of straw or earth. This involves three simple steps: 1) Dig the earth in front and back of the plant. 2) With the foot or fork gently push the plant down to the ground. 3) Cover lightly with mulch, straw, or earth. In the dry season make sure there is adequate moisture to carry the plant through the winter months.

Proverbs 27:12 tells us: *"A prudent man foresees evil and hides himself; the simple pass on and are punished."* A wise boy or girl looks ahead with the end in mind. They will prepare themselves to be adults by centering their youth with Christ's life. Jesus invites, *"Take my yoke upon you, and learn of me; for I am meek and lowly in heart: and ye shall find rest unto your souls. For my yoke is easy, and my burden is light"* (Matthew 11:29, 30). Yoked up with Jesus we go where He goes and do not go where He will not. He will protect us from "wild oat" sowing in youth! We may reap Jesus both now in youth and then as adults!

PRACTICAL PROJECT

As a family, walk around your house and note what special care has been taken in order for nature to be ready for winter. What can a family do to be ready for winter? What food, clothes, or house preparation needs to be done before winter? The Bible warns of a coming "time of trouble such as never was since there was a nation" (Daniel 12:1). What preparation is needed to be ready for this end time, last days storm? Do we need to move our home to a safer place like in the country where we might grow our own food?

Grow Protected

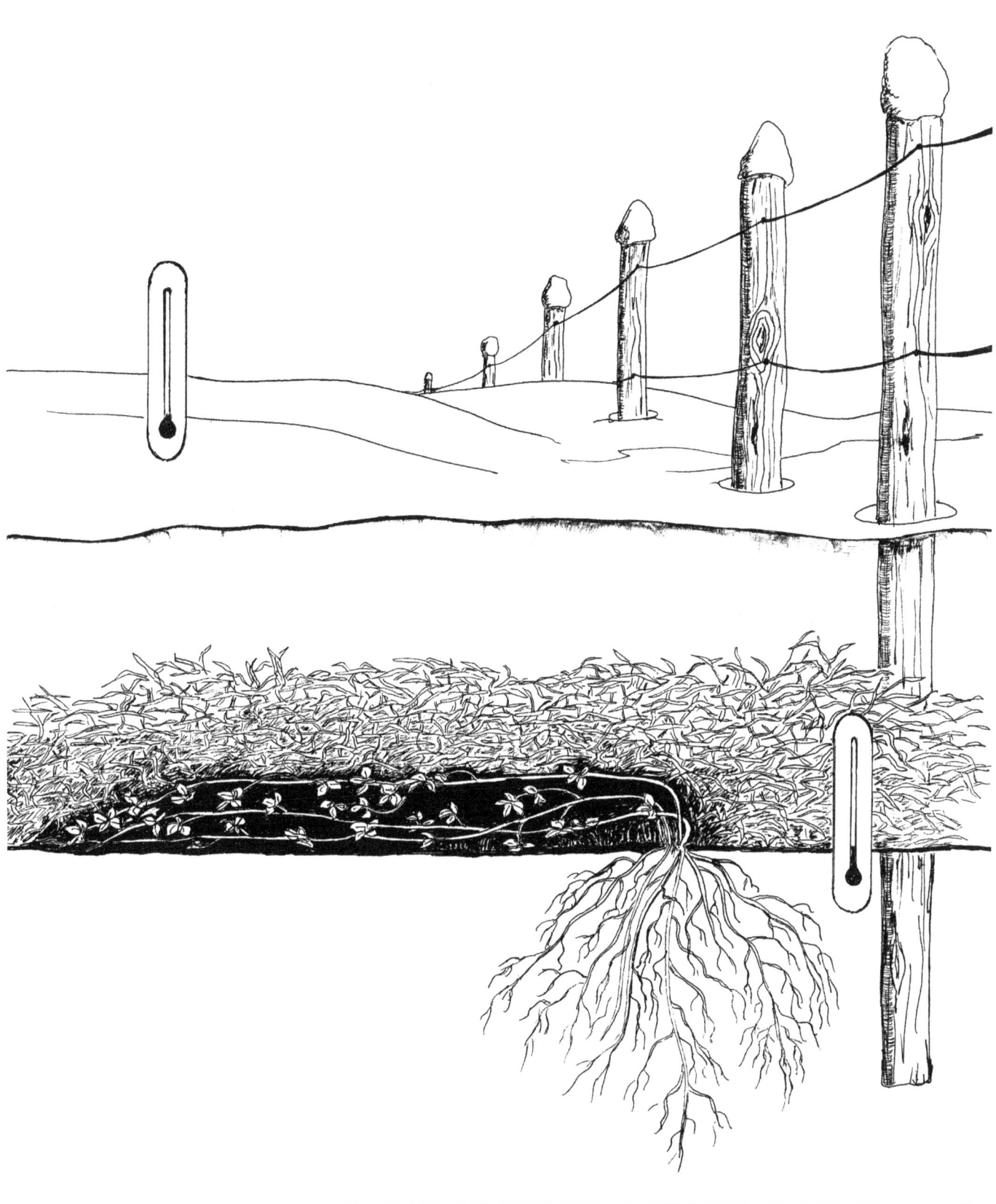

Enemies of Blackberries

Blackberries have many visible and invisible enemies that cripple, weaken, or kill the plant. These pests all drain energy and resources that weaken or destroy the ability to bear fruit.

Several insect pests **attack the leaves**, such as Japanese Beatle or Red Humpel caterpillars. They and their children eat leaves, cutting off the plants' energy source. Fungus spores like orange rust harm the leaves. Our energy sources come via our five senses. We must continually guard them to take in the good and block the bad.

Some **attack the canes** like cane borers or San Jose scale. They weaken the plants' ability to deliver food and energy to the leaves and fruit. Our body delivers energy via our blood to all 100 trillion cells bringing food and carrying out the waste. We must guard our health so they can do this for us.

Others **attack the roots** like Crown Root Galls affecting the water and nutrient supplies. These are invisible, hiding underground. Nematodes also wreck great loss at the root level. We are to be "rooted and grounded in Christ." Satan always attacks this root.

Others are **totally invisible** like sterility (a symptom of a virus), which grows vigorous plants, but sets no fruit or produces deformed berries. Satan hates the truth of spiritual fruits. He has an invisible lie for each one.

Alert attentiveness is needed to catch these pests at the beginning stage and remove them from your garden.

Jesus warns: *"An enemy has done this"* (Matthew 13:28). *"Just as through one man, sin entered the world, and death through sin, thus death spread to all men"* (Romans 5:12). Man's lawlessness (sin) has infected the whole natural world beside himself. *"For we know that the whole creation groans and labors with birth pangs together until now"* (Romans 8:20). When Adam surrendered his will to the lawless rebel Satan, this fallen mighty intelligence then perverted every good creation to some lawless or destructive activity.

PRACTICAL PROJECT

Look at nature around your home. Do you see signs of pests and disease? Do we find evidence that "all creation groans to be delivered"? How can we help nature recover? What about our homes, spiritually? We don't need to cultivate his lies, but exterminate them by God's grace and Truth.

Enemies of Blackberries

Was it Worth It?

Luther Burbank lived seventy-seven satisfying years of life. He continually tried to be useful. "Time cannot be added to a person's life, but it can be made more valuable by avoiding waste," was his philosophy. When he was sixty-three years old he had created and introduced for our use 222 new varieties of trees, vegetables, fruits, and flowers. He introduced 250 new varieties on about 50 different classes of plants. He tried more experiments which failed than those which succeeded. The wisdom he learned was that failure is just a step towards success.

At Burbank's 10-acre Sebastopol Farm, I stood by one old apple tree which had 526 varieties still growing on it. There usually were more than a million plants growing on his 10 acres, and he always had at least 3,000 different experiments going at the same time. It was his absolute belief in the law of the farm— "sow what you reap"—that enabled him to faithfully, persistently work and to bless our hungry world with the harvest fruits of his life.

God so loved our (demon possessed) world that He sent his only Son to "crossbreed" into selfish humanity His own divine love. The Son of God humbled himself to become the Son of Man. The "seed of woman," the "seed of Abraham," the "seed of David."

He became one cell in Mary's womb. For thirty years "Immanuel" ate, slept, and walked among His chosen people. He fed 5,000, calmed storms, healed the sick and raised the dead. But they would not believe He was the Son of God. It was for this crime ("if you're the Son of God"), that He was crucified between two thieves. It was on the cross He drained the last drops of "everlasting love" for our ungrateful hearts. He died the second death, to pay our debt of sin. By faith in the law of the farm, He gave us His all, believing we would respond to His love and, receiving it, we would reap His unselfish eternal love and life.

Knowledge is progressive. So is love. With it, reverence and happiness increase. The more we learn of God, the greater will be our admiration of His character. The great controversy between "thorn" and "fruit" is ended. Sin and sinners are no more. The entire universe is clean. Like Burbank's bonfire, God's fire has cleaned and removed all that offends. From Him who created all, stream life and light and gladness throughout the realms of illimitable space. From the minutest atom to the greatest world, all things, animate and inanimate, in their unshadowed beauty and perfect joy, sing and declare that God is love. "That the love wherewith thou hast loved me may be in them, and I in them" (John 17:26). From the Creator's point of view, you were worth it all.

PRACTICAL PROJECT

As a family, purpose to read from God's "seed catalog," the Bible, every morning and evening. Let us daily cultivate His divine best, and by the Holy Spirit destroy the rest. Let us experience His everlasting love every day.

Was it Worth It?

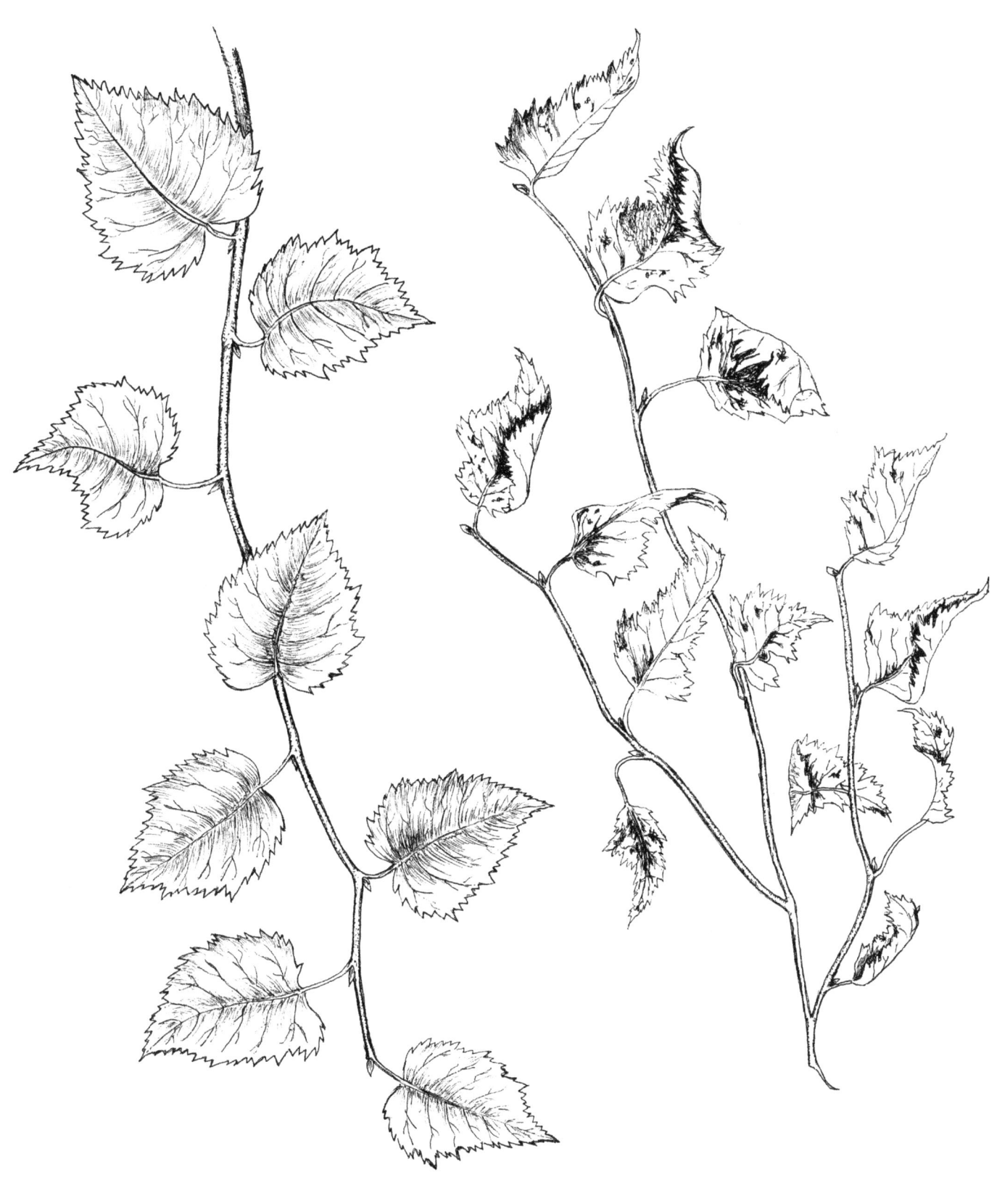

APPENDIX A—The Tree of Life

This book reveals how Burbank used the invisible law of genetics, created on day three, to remove the curse of sin (thorns) from blackberries. Using the same law for 30 years, he cultivated fruit till he finally reaped what he sowed. Faithfully working this one law he took blackberries all the way back to Genesis 1—full delicious fruit on thornless bushes!

On our original perfect planet grew two trees. "And out of the ground made the Lord God to grow every tree that is pleasant to the sight, and good for food; the tree of life also in the midst of the garden, and the tree of knowledge of good and evil" (Genesis 2:9). Both trees were planted by God. As trees, each had roots, trunk, limbs, leaves and fruit. Let us consider the tree of life first. On the next page we will look at the tree of good and evil.

God's Law, the Ten Commandments of Exodus 20, is illustrated as the tree of life upon which are growing the fruits of the Spirit we have just studied in the preceding pages. God's law is divided by two great "limbs." The first "limb" shows us how to love God first. From Him we find a love that teaches us how we are to relate to each other (the second "limb" on the right). God wrote this Law on two tablets of stone, on front and back of each tablet (see Exodus 32:15, 16). On the front side of tablet one is how we are to love God only, and not to use idols or images in our worship of Him. On the back of this tablet there are two more limbs: reverence His name and reverence His day. Reverence His day by working six days as He did, and not working on the seventh day, Saturday. He rested on this day from His work of creation.

The second great "limb" is the other tablet—how we love each other. It has two limbs; on the front side it is all about life. God gave us life through our parents who created us. That right to life is to continue and is to be passed on by reproduction. This process is protected by faithfulness (no adultery). On the back of this tablet are three more limbs regarding what we do with life. The right to ownership of the work of our hands, and the right to truth—no lies or deceptions. Third, being grateful, without coveting what someone else has.

This tree's root motivation is God's everlasting love. There is no law against this tree's commands—the fruits of the spirit that grow here—they are all about love.

PRACTICAL PROJECT

Make a copy of the Ten Commandments on two tablets. On one tablet, write on the front the first two commands. On the back side write down commandments three and four. Why are the two longest commandments found, one on the front, and one on the back of this tablet?

On the second tablet on the front, write down commandments five, six and seven. How are these three all about "life"? On the back, write down the remaining commandments eight, nine and ten. Place your copy of this law in a very visible place, for "It is your life and length of days" (Deuteronomy 32:47). "It is the law of liberty" (James 2:12). "Love, everlasting love, is how this law is fulfilled" (Romans 13:10). Love grows here.

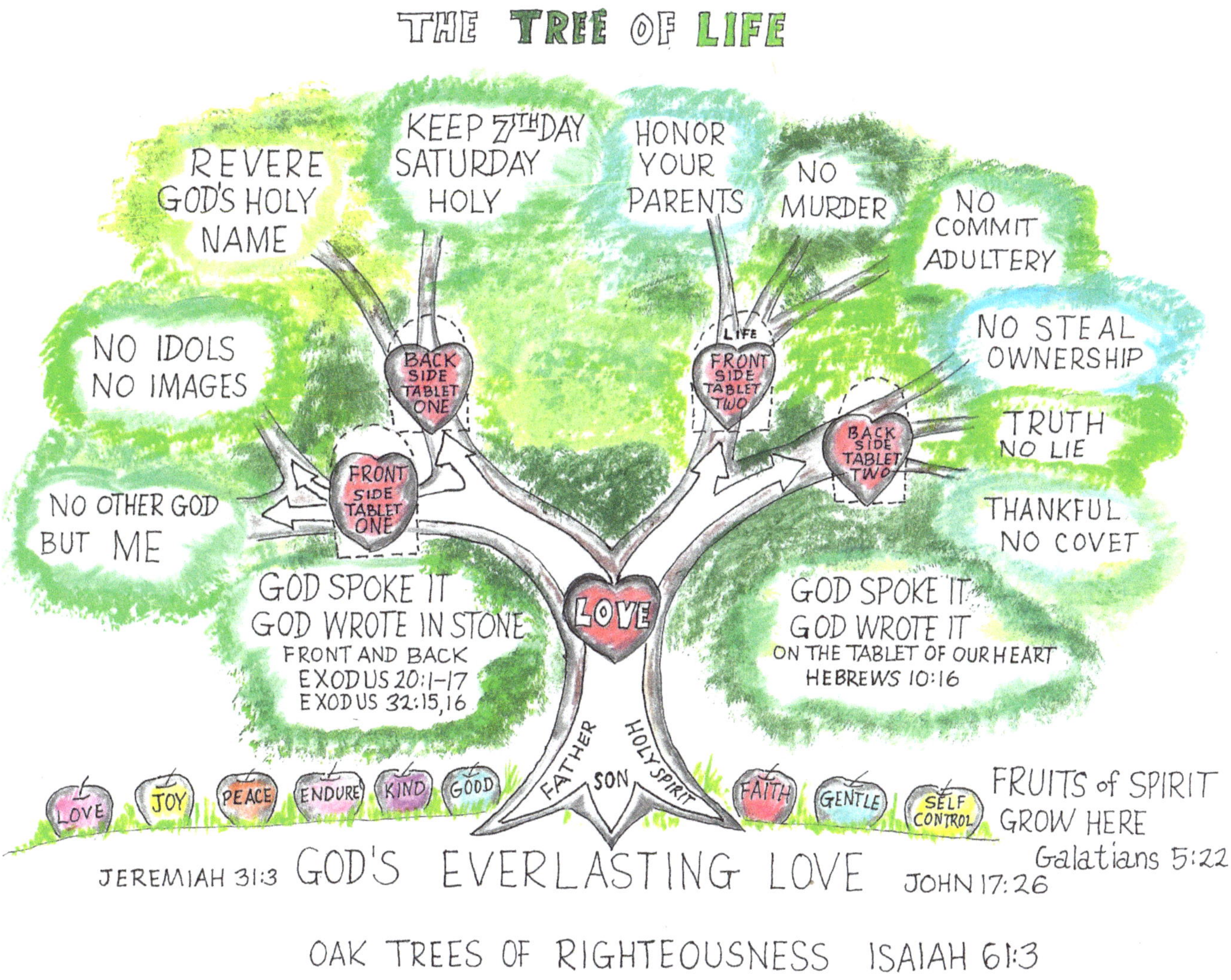

APPENDIX A—The Tree of Life

THE TREE OF LIFE

- REVERE GOD'S HOLY NAME
- KEEP 7TH DAY SATURDAY HOLY
- HONOR YOUR PARENTS
- NO MURDER
- NO COMMIT ADULTERY
- NO IDOLS NO IMAGES
- NO STEAL OWNERSHIP
- TRUTH NO LIE
- NO OTHER GOD BUT ME
- THANKFUL NO COVET

BACK SIDE TABLET ONE
FRONT SIDE TABLET ONE
FRONT SIDE TABLET TWO — LIFE
BACK SIDE TABLET TWO
LOVE

GOD SPOKE IT GOD WROTE IN STONE
FRONT AND BACK
EXODUS 20:1-17
EXODUS 32:15,16

GOD SPOKE IT GOD WROTE IT
ON THE TABLET OF OUR HEART
HEBREWS 10:16

FATHER — SON — HOLY SPIRIT

Fruits: LOVE, JOY, PEACE, ENDURE, KIND, GOOD, FAITH, GENTLE, SELF CONTROL

FRUITS of SPIRIT GROW HERE
Galatians 5:22

JEREMIAH 31:3   GOD'S EVERLASTING LOVE   JOHN 17:26

OAK TREES OF RIGHTEOUSNESS   ISAIAH 61:3

APPENDIX B—Tree of Good and Evil—The Tree of Hate

In the beginning this tree looked like the Tree of Life we just studied on the previous page. The tree on this page reveals the harvest of evil, the forbidden knowledge God did not want us to know. What was this forbidden knowledge? God did not want us to know fear, guilt, and worry.

So dangerous is the mix of good and evil, called Academic Freedom, the right to know evil. Solomon tried this tree and the book of Ecclesiastes is the result. He said: *"All is vanity!"* (Ecclesiastes 1:2).

"Let no one deceive you"; "the heart is deceitful above all things, and desperately wicked"; "Can the Ethiopian change his skin or the leopard his spots" (Ephesians 5:6; Jeremiah 17:9; 13:23). "With a double heart do they speak" (Psalm 12:2); "Deceit is in the heart of them that imagine evil" (Proverbs 12:20). David prayed, "Create in me a clean heart" (Psalm 51:10). "Keep the heart with all diligence; for out of it are the issues of life" (Proverbs 4:23). James 1:26 says, "We can deceive our own heart."

When we look at the "live only for the now" limb of this tree, it is the worship of self as a god and final authority. It is the Serpent's first teaching, "ye shall be as gods" (Genesis 3:5). Spiritism teaches self is the final authority, desire is your only rule. One can worship as many idols as you serve and seek. God's name is used as a curse word. And Sunday is a human "works" substitute for the Creator's rest day, Saturday, the Sabbath.

On the "violent competitive" relationship limb, every person is someone to beat, coerce, or hate. This may even go to the point of removal by killing them. Sex is all about what pleases me, so there are many options to please self.

Ownership is all about who has the most and best, and I'll get it all by theft or lying because of jealousy or envy. Worry and fear are the way of life, worry that someone bigger or smarter will rob me of what is mine. This is our world today. This book is about the most fundamental law of life: "sowing and reaping."

🌿 PRACTICAL PROJECT

Jesus taught us to pray, "deliver us from evil" (Mathew 6:13). As a family, discuss how the "tree of good and evil" gets into our home. What mediums bring their "mix" of good and evil? DVDs? Smartphones? Computer games? Magazines? Books? Music? Internet? "Be not deceived, God is not mocked: for whatsoever a man soweth, that shall he also reap. For he that soweth to his flesh shall of the flesh reap corruption; but he that soweth to the Spirit shall of the Spirit reap life everlasting" (Galatians 6:7,8).

APPENDIX B—Tree of Good and Evil—The Tree of Hate

APPENDIX C—Bibliography

The Christian Doctrine of Sanctification Considered in Eight Sermons, by Edward Garrard Marsh, preached before the University of Oxford, at the Bampton Lecture, for the year 1847.

Luther Burbank Plant Magician, by John Beaty. Julian Messner, inc. New York, 1943.

A book worth reading to your children.

Luther Burbank was born March 7, 1849, on a farm near Lancaster, Massachusetts. He felt time was a gift of the Creator to be used to the fullest extent and he lived a happy seventy-seven years. He continually tried to be useful. He considered his time to be worth a hundred dollars a minute.

He moved to Santa Rosa, Californa in 1875 and later bought a farm seven miles away near Sebastopol. Here, at 36 years of age, he began his work as a plant inventor full time. He was self taught using his eyes, smell, and taste to very carefully observe what nature was doing. He never specialized but worked with many different kinds of plants. He often had over 3,000 experiments going at the same time. He considered every problem one step closer to success. He failed at more experiments than the ones that succeeded. His faithful persistence brought him fame.

There were usually more than a million plants growing on his ten acres. Here he had a world laboratory, getting plants from all over the world.

In his personal life, he did not consider himself a Christian for he never found a church that taught what he observed, but he did believe there was a Creator. He married twice, his first ended in divorce. He never had any children of his own. No matter how busy he was, he would stop and wave to the children who called out to him passing his farm. As a world-famous man he was timid and shy.

When asked to speak to a nearby school on his birthday, he asked his helper to speak for him. "Tell the boys and girls I love them. Tell them I know they will become good men and women. Tell them this is a beautiful world full of wonders. Tell them to look for interesting things and they will never have a dull moment. Tell them to learn how to use what they find. Tell them to have faith and confidence. Who knows, one of them may do all that I have done, and more."

APPENDIX C—Bibliography

 APPENDIX D—The Law of the Farm

Burbank was sometimes accused of using Darwin's theory of evolution: "The Survival of the Fittest." But this was not true. Darwin taught it was natural unguided selection that created all of life. Burbank's method was the opposite of "natural selection". He very carefully selected the qualities he wanted to develop, and he chose the "best" he wished to grow. Using this method he developed thornless cactus, plums with small pits and large flesh, thornless blackberry, including a white blackberry, just to name a few.

What Burbank proved was, the law of genetics is absolutely sure. And he faithfully, persistently used this law to work his wonders.

He proved and demonstrated the truth of Galatians 6:7–9. He was not deceived.

"Be not deceived; God is not mocked: for whatsoever a man soweth, that shall he also reap" (Galatians 6:7–9). This fundamental law God created on day three for the creation of all life: "After its kind" (Genesis 1:11). After its kind is mentioned 11 times in Genesis 1. This is the law of genetics. It was this law that made redemption possible. "For he that soweth to his flesh shall of the flesh reap corruption; but he that soweth to the Spirit shall of the spirit reap life everlasting. And let us not be weary in well doing; for in due season we shall reap, if we faint not" (Galatians 6:8, 9).

Jesus was "the seed of the woman" of Genesis 3:15. He demonstrated that fallen humanity could perfectly live the law of love, when united with the Father. When we are united with Jesus, His divinity will prove the same. We are his witness that His divine "seed" will create everlasting love forever.

APPENDIX D—The Law of the Farm

Subscribe to the Leading Bible-based Nature Journal!

Readers call it, "The Christian answer to National Geographic!"

- Stunning Photography
- Animal & Bird Features
- Creation Science
- Outdoor Travel Adventures
- Gardening Tips
- Youth Photo & Coloring Contests
- Character-building Lessons found in Nature
- Instructional Study Guide
- Even Genesis Cuisine Recipes for healthful living!

UNPLUG and Get Away to Nature & Creation!

4 Quarterly Issues Only $19.95/year–INCLUDES a FREE Digital Subscription
ORDER NOW!
Logon to: www.CreationIllustrated.com or Call: 1(800) 360-2732
or Mail a Check to: Creation Illustrated, PO Box 141103, Spokane Valley, WA 99214

The Gospel According to Creation Seminars

Terry McComb, Speaker and Writer with *Creation Illustrated* magazine, has conducted countless character-building, Bible-based seminars that reveal eternal truths through the handiwork of God. The Spiritual messages have a lasting impact on all ages and include blacklight chalk drawings with his wife's soft piano artistry in the background.

Pastor McComb has authored more than 50 articles with *Creation Illustrated* magazine and co-authored with his wife Jean, five children's books for parents to study with their children—*Gospel According to a Dandelion; Gospel According to a Blade of Grass; Gospel According to a Snowflake; Gospel According to a Thornless Blackberry;* and *Gospel According to a Tree.*

Available Seminars (available for purchase as a digital download or DVD copy):

"The Creation Story" is a scientific walk through Genesis one. How does each day of the Creation Week reveal its Author and how is this truth relevant to our spiritual walk? A nine-hour seminar from Sunday through Saturday night.

"In His Image" focuses on the wonder of the human body! This nine-hour seminar is a fast-moving study that examines the 12 systems of the body and their amazing designer. Deeply scientific, yet spiritual.

"The Wonder of a Tree" is a nine-hour seminar illustrating how the lifestyle, function, and ways of a tree reveal the ways of its Creator, Jesus Christ.

"Creations Creator" is a five-hour week-end seminar that addresses evolution vs. creation and the truth about Dinosaurs. Topics include: The Cross as Seen in Nature, Worship Him Who Made, Heart Reading Nature, and the Gospel According to a Dandelion power point presentation with music background.

"How to Heart Read Nature" will help viewers learn how to see past the trees and see the Creator. This is a hands-on practical nine-hour seminar that uses the out-of-doors classroom and needs to be in a nature setting. Short on theory and long on active learning.

"The Heavens are Telling" deals with The Gospel According to Astronomy" with plenty of NASA space telescope photos. This nine-hour seminar shows God's ways in outer space to help fill your heart's inner space with His love.

These Seminars can be done by Zoom
To Book a Seminar or order books and DVD's
Call: (250) 547-6696
E-mail: terry@gospelcreation.com
Web site: www.gospelcreation.com
Write: The Gospel According to Creation Seminar
39 Pine Road, Cherryville, British Columbia, Canada V0E 2G3

TEACH Services, Inc.
P U B L I S H I N G

We invite you to view the complete
selection of titles we publish at:
www.TEACHServices.com

We encourage you to write us
with your thoughts about this,
or any other book we publish at:
info@TEACHServices.com

TEACH Services' titles may be purchased in
bulk quantities for educational, fund-raising,
business, or promotional use.
bulksales@TEACHServices.com

Finally, if you are interested in seeing
your own book in print, please contact us at:
publishing@TEACHServices.com

We are happy to review your manuscript at no charge.

www.ingramcontent.com/pod-product-compliance
Lightning Source LLC
Chambersburg PA
CBHW061603170426
43196CB00039B/2967